# Antarctica

**MEL FRIEDMAN**

**Children's Press®**
An Imprint of Scholastic Inc.
New York  Toronto  London  Auckland  Sydney
Mexico City  New Delhi  Hong Kong
Danbury, Connecticut

**Content Consultant**
Judy Diamond, Ph.D.
Professor and Curator
University of Nebraska State Museum
University of Nebraska
Lincoln, NE

Library of Congress Cataloging-in-Publication Data

Friedman, Mel, 1946-
 Antarctica / by Mel Friedman.
        p. cm. -- (A true book)
 Includes index.
     ISBN-13: 978-0-531-16864-6 (lib. bdg.)
                 978-0-531-21826-6 (pbk.)
     ISBN-10: 0-531-16864-6 (lib. bdg.)
                 0-531-21826-0 (pbk.)

 1. Antarctica--Juvenile literature. I. Title. II. Series.

 G863.F75 2008
 919.8'9--dc22

 2007050253

Produced by Weldon Owen Education Inc.

©2009 Scholastic Inc.

1 2 3 4 5 6 7 8 9 10 R 18 17 16 15 14 13 12 11 10 09

# Find the Truth!

**Everything** you are about to read is true *except* for one of the sentences on this page.

Which one is **TRUE**?

T or F    Polar bears live farther south than any other mammal.

T or F    Antarctica's size changes according to the season of the year.

Find the answers in this book.

3

# Contents

# THE BIG TRUTH!

## Fire and Ice

What happens when hot steam freezes? . . . . . . . **28**

In 2000, an iceberg the size of Connecticut broke free from Antarctica.

The world's largest icebergs break off from Antarctica. Chinstrap penguins sometimes breed on icebergs.

# CHAPTER 1

# The Extreme Continent

Welcome to Antarctica—the coldest, driest, windiest, iciest continent! A person's breath can freeze in an instant. Winds can be stronger than a hurricane's. Plants are scarce. The largest native land animal is an insect. In this harsh **climate**, almost everything is covered with ice and snow.

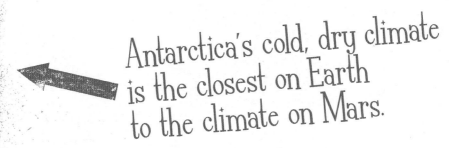

Antarctica's cold, dry climate is the closest on Earth to the climate on Mars.

# Arctic's Opposite

Antarctica is the southernmost region on Earth. In fact, *Antarctica* means "the land opposite the Arctic." The continent lies entirely in the **Southern Hemisphere**. At its icy heart is the South Pole. This is Earth's southernmost point. Antarctica is the fifth-largest continent. It is about one and a half times the size of the United States.

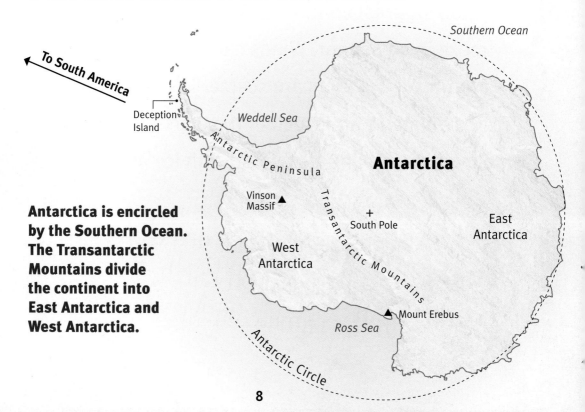

**Antarctica is encircled by the Southern Ocean. The Transantarctic Mountains divide the continent into East Antarctica and West Antarctica.**

To South America

Deception Island

Weddell Sea

Antarctic Peninsula

Southern Ocean

Vinson Massif ▲

**Antarctica**

Transantarctic Mountains

+ South Pole

East Antarctica

West Antarctica

▲ Mount Erebus

Ross Sea

Antarctic Circle

# Highs and Lows

The crushing weight of Antarctica's ice pushes down some parts of the land to 8,380 feet (2,555 meters) below sea level. Some of Antarctica's mountains are completely buried under ice. Antarctica's highest mountain is the Vinson Massif. It rises to 16,066 feet (4,897 meters) above sea level.

Vinson Massif

Inland Antarctica is drier than
the Sahara Desert in Africa.

# CHAPTER 2

# Ice Desert

Antarctica is considered a desert. That is because it is so dry. Inland, it never rains and seldom snows. All but two percent of the land lies under thick sheets of ice. One enormous sheet covers East Antarctica. Another covers West Antarctica. The Transantarctic Mountain range separates these sheets. It is 2,200 miles (3,500 kilometers) long.

In some Antarctic valleys, it has not rained for more than two million years!

**Volcano on Deception Island, Antarctica**

Antarctica has at least two active volcanoes.

# Under the Ice

The ice on the Antarctic sheets is freshwater, not saltwater. The sheets formed over millions of years from layers of snow that never melted. They contain about 90 percent of the world's ice. That's nearly three-quarters of all the freshwater in the world! The ice sheet covering East Antarctica is at least 14 million years old.

Antarctica is the world's highest continent. Its ice sheets are as thick as 11,500 feet (3,505 meters) in places. Antarctica has some of the world's biggest glaciers. These are formed when snow turns to ice over time. These masses of ice begin to flow under the pressure of their own weight. When a glacier reaches the sea, chunks of ice sometimes break off, forming icebergs.

The birth of an iceberg from a glacier is called calving.

# Wild and Windy Weather

Antarctica holds the record for the world's lowest temperature: −128.6 °F (−89.2 °C). In some places, it is too cold for snow. Tiny ice crystals fall instead. They are known as "diamond dust."

Seawater freezes at a lower temperature than freshwater. Yet every winter, sea ice forms around Antarctica. Also, snow and ice on the continent form **ice shelves**. These extend into the sea from the ice sheets. These cause Antarctica to double in size.

**Most ships visit Antarctica in summer, when the sea ice is not so dense.**

14

Auroras, seen here above a British research station, are produced by solar wind.

Because Antarctica is in the Southern Hemisphere, summer begins in December. Winter begins in June. At the South Pole, the sun never sets in summer and never rises in winter.

Wind speeds of up to 200 miles per hour (322 kilometers per hour) have been clocked in Antarctica. Fierce gusts, called **katabatic** (ka-tuh-BA-tik) winds, often create blizzards.

In the Antarctic night sky, there are sometimes colorful displays of light. These are the southern lights, or **auroras** (au-ROH-ruhs).

Seals spend most of their
time on sea ice and in the sea.
They go ashore only to breed
and raise their young.

# CHAPTER 3

# Life in the Cold Zone

Survival on Antarctica is tough. Living things must be able to cope with both the harsh climate and months of darkness. Few plants and animals can live on land there year round. The Southern Ocean, however, is full of life. Many animals, such as whales, also come to Antarctica in the summer to feed.

Weddell (wi-DELL) seals live farther south than any other mammal.

# Tiny Plants, Tiny Animals

Most plant life in Antarctica is **lichens**, mosses, **algae**, and **liverworts**. These plants may cling to rock or thrive in snowmelt. Some even live inside ice! A grass and a tiny flowering plant are the only native higher plant forms. These live on the Antarctic **Peninsula**. This peninsula is close to South America. It is warmer and wetter than the rest of Antarctica. Temperatures can rise to above freezing in summer.

Most native Antarctic land animals are insects or mites that are related to spiders. (There are no polar bears in Antarctica!) The largest native land-dweller is the eyeless, wingless springtail. This insect is about half an inch (13 millimeters) long. In spring and summer, birds come to Antarctica to breed. Only the emperor penguin remains on the continent through the winter.

Grass grows on sunny slopes in Antarctica. Albatrosses come ashore to breed.

# In the Sea

Sea animals thrive in Antarctica. Whales are summer visitors. However, many kinds of seals, dolphins, fish, squid, and jellyfish live there year round. Several Antarctic fish have a kind of antifreeze in their blood. It keeps them from freezing solid.

At the bottom of the Antarctic food chain is a one-celled plant. It is called a **diatom**. In summer, diatom blooms provide a feast for krill, a tiny shrimp-like creature. In turn, krill is an essential protein food for many fish, birds, and sea mammals.

**Sea spiders as large as 12 inches (30 centimeters) across live in Antarctic waters.**

**In winter, humpback whales leave Antarctica. Many of them head to the east coast of Australia to have their young.**

A humpback whale eats about one and a half tons of krill in one day!

## Passing Through

More than ten different kinds of whales come to Antarctica in summer to feed. In winter, they head north to warmer waters. They leave to breed or to give birth to their young. Newborn whales would not survive in the icy waters of Antarctica.

# Millions of Birds

Many kinds of birds begin life on Antarctica. Some spend their lives there. About 40 kinds of seabirds breed in Antarctica in the summer. These include albatrosses, cormorants, terns, and gulls. More than 15 kinds of penguins live in Antarctica. Penguins are found only in the Southern Hemisphere. They cannot fly. But they are expert swimmers. They can dive hundreds of feet in search of food.

**The Kelp Gull is the only type of gull in Antarctica.**

# King-Sized

The biggest penguin in the world is the emperor penguin. It grows to be about four feet (1.2 meters) tall. It is the only penguin that breeds in the Antarctic winter. It raises its young in the harshest conditions on Earth. First the female lays an egg. Then the male rests the egg, and later the chick, on its feet. This keeps the chick off the ice. The father's warm belly warms the chick. In storms, the penguins huddle in groups of as many as 5,000. To keep warm, they take turns moving from the outside to the inside.

Icebergs appear white because the ice is full of bubbles. Blue streaks are clear, bubble-free ice. These result when ice in cracks refreezes.

# CHAPTER 4

# Mysterious Land

The ancient Greeks were the first to suggest that an unknown continent lay south of the equator. They imagined this land to be warm and fertile. Explorers did not venture into the Southern Ocean until the 1700s. The ice and extreme weather would keep them off the continent for nearly 100 more years.

Between 50 and 99 percent of an iceberg is under the water.

# The Southern Search

In 1768, the British government sent Captain James Cook to search for a southern continent. In 1773, Cook sailed farther south than any explorer before him. He crossed into Antarctic waters. He then sailed around the whole continent. He never sighted land. Sea ice stopped him from getting close enough. However, his voyage proved one thing. If there really were a southern continent, it would be too far south to be habitable.

The Ross Ice Shelf is about the size of France. Where it meets the sea, its cliffs are nearly 200 feet (61 meters) high.

# Chasing a Continent

In the 1800s, Antarctic exploration was pursued by naval officers, whalers, and sealers from many nations. No one knows for sure who was the first to sight land or set foot on Antarctica itself.

In 1841, James C. Ross, a British naval officer, went beyond the Antarctic sea ice. He entered what is now the Ross Sea and mapped its coast. He discovered the Ross Ice Shelf and Mount Erebus, an active volcano.

Crater

# Fire and Ice

Mount Erebus is the southernmost active volcano in the world. It has been active continuously since 1972. It spits out as many as 50 lava bombs a day. Some of them are as big as 10 feet (three meters) across.

## Lava Lake

The lava in most volcanoes is hidden under a cap of solid rock, until it spews out during an eruption. Mount Erebus has a lake of steaming lava in the crater at its summit. This offers scientists the rare opportunity to study lava firsthand.

## Hot Spots

Hot gas seeping through the sides of the volcano forms caves in the ice. It is warm and humid inside the caves. Steam escaping from the caves freezes instantly. It forms towers of ice as tall as 60 feet (18.3 meters). There are hundreds of these towers on Mount Erebus.

29

Robert Scott made his second trip to Antarctica on the ship *Terra Nova*. The name is Latin for "new land."

# The Great Race

The years 1897–1917 are often called the "heroic era" of Antarctic exploration. There were 15 scientific expeditions to Antarctica during this period. But the great historic event was the race to the South Pole. Two brave explorers competed with each other to be first to accomplish this goal.

Since 1991, non-native animals are no longer permitted in Antarctica.

# Amundsen's Dreams

Roald Amundsen (1872–1928) was the son of a Norwegian shipowner. His dream was to be a famous explorer. He quit medical studies as a young man and went to sea. In 1905, he pioneered a sea route through the Arctic ice. In 1909, he was planning an expedition to the North Pole. After hearing that others had beat him to it, he decided to be the first to make it to the South Pole instead.

Amundsen had studied the ways of native peoples of the Arctic. He learned how to work with sled dogs. He also learned how to dress for the cold. He used skis and dog sleds for his Antarctic expedition.

# Great Scott

Robert Falcon Scott (1868–1912) joined the British Navy when he was thirteen. From 1901 to 1904, he commanded a British expedition to Antarctica. The expedition reached farther south than had any before it. Scott returned to Britain a national hero. In 1910, he was sent on another expedition to Antarctica. This time, the goal was to reach the South Pole.

**Scott was a poor skier. He had no experience with sled dogs. He used ponies, motorized vehicles, and manpower to pull the sleds.**

# Brave Efforts

In the fall of 1911, both Scott's and Amundsen's teams set out to reach the South Pole. They had to cross about 800 miles (1,300 kilometers) of snow and dangerous ice. Scott reached the pole on January 17, 1912. The Norwegian flag was already there. Amundsen had beat him by 34 days. Scott and his men were disappointed and worn out. On the return journey, tragedy struck. They were hit by extreme weather. For weeks, they struggled on, but all five men died.

## Antarctic Time Line

### 1840

French explorer Jules d'Urville names the penguins he sees in East Antarctica after his wife, Adélie.

### 1911

Norwegian explorer Roald Amundsen is the first person to reach the South Pole.

# Living Memorial

Eight months later, the tent and frozen bodies of Scott and two of his men were found. Scott's diary gave the public a firsthand account of their tragedy. It quickly became a best seller.

The hut that Scott used on his first Antarctic expedition is still there. It has been preserved as a museum. To step inside it is to step back 100 years. Food, utensils, and gear are all there, as if waiting to be used. The hut serves as a memorial to all the explorers of the heroic era.

**1929**
Richard E. Byrd of the U.S. Navy is the first person to fly to the South Pole.

**1959**
The Antarctic Treaty is signed. It dedicates the continent to nonmilitary uses and to science.

**Will Steger's team endured extreme conditions crossing Antarctica. Sometimes blowing snow would almost suffocate them when they gulped for air.**

# CHAPTER 6

# Modern Explorers

Since the heroic era, there have been many expeditions to Antarctica. A few have carried on the grand heroic tradition. In 1989–1990, for example, American Will Steger led the first dogsled crossing of Antarctica. It covered more than 3,700 miles (6,000 kilometers) and took seven months.

Will Steger's team had a dog trainer specifically to care for its 36 sled dogs.

# Researching Antarctica

Antarctica is not only the coldest and driest place on Earth. It is also the cleanest! Its environment has been stable for millions of years. This makes it a great place for scientists. They study diatom fossils for valuable information about Antarctica's climate history. They study ice and land to learn about Earth's origins.

Most research in Antarctica is done in summer. About one quarter of the people stay there through the winter.

The polar regions play a special role in the world's climate. Ice and snow are like giant reflectors. They bounce the sun's rays back into space. This keeps Earth cool enough to live on.

There is a thin layer of **ozone** gas in Earth's atmosphere. It blocks harmful **ultraviolet light** from the sun. In the 1980s, scientists discovered a hole in this layer, right above Antarctica. Thanks to research, steps are now being taken to ensure that the ozone hole closes up again.

Bacteria and viruses do not thrive outdoors in Antarctica. Food doesn't spoil. People don't catch colds easily.

# Leading Ladies

Women have been actively involved in Antarctic research and exploration since 1969. In 1974, Dr. Mary Alice McWhinnie was the first woman to be named chief scientist of the U.S. McMurdo Station. In 1992, American Ann Bancroft led the first women's team to the South Pole on skis. In 1994, Liv Arnesen of Norway became the first woman to ski alone to the South Pole.

**Liv Arnesen in Antarctica**

# Poles Apart

The geographic South Pole is the southern point around which Earth spins. The magnetic South Pole is the spot toward which the south end of all compass needles points. It is more than 1,678 miles (2,700) kilometers away from the geographic pole. It shifts several miles each year. Earth's magnetic field reverses direction about once every 500,000 years. When this happens, the North and South magnetic poles swap places!

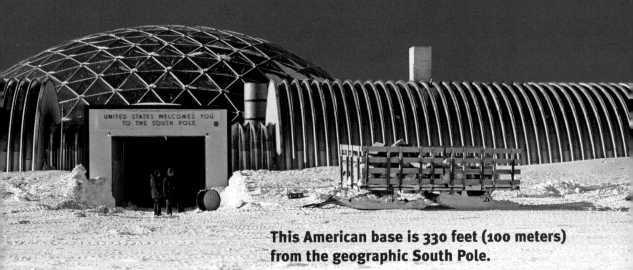

UNITED STATES WELCOMES YOU
TO THE SOUTH POLE

**This American base is 330 feet (100 meters) from the geographic South Pole.**

# A Special Place

In 1959, the Antarctic Treaty was signed. Antarctica became the only place in the world shared solely for peaceful, scientific study. In 2007, some 60 countries launched the International Polar Year (IPY). Scientists used it to study Earth's polar regions, to better understand our planet. ★

**This South Pole was set up for tourist photos. Every year, as the ice shifts, it moves several feet away from the geographic South Pole.**

# True Statistics

**Population of Antarctica in summer:**
About 4,000 scientists; 25,000 tourists

**Population of Antarctica in winter:**
About 1,000 scientists

**Total land area:** About 5.4 million square miles (14 million square kilometers)

**Total ice-free land area:** About 17,330 square miles (44,890 square kilometers)

**Average winter temperature at the South Pole:** −76 °F (−60 °C)

**Average summer temperature at the South Pole:** −17.5 °F (−27.5 °C)

## Did you find the truth?

**F** Polar bears live farther south than any other mammal.

**T** Antarctica's size changes according to the season of the year.

# Resources

## Books

Bredeson, Carmen. *After the Last Dog Died: The True-Life, Hair-Raising Adventure of Douglas Mawson and His 1911–1914 Antarctic Expedition.* Des Moines, IA: National Geographic Children's Books, 2003.

Cerullo, Mary M. *Life Under Ice.* Gardiner, ME: Tilbury House Publishers, 2005.

Karner, Julie. *Roald Amundsen: The Conquest of the South Pole* (In the Footsteps of Explorers). New York: Crabtree Publishing Company, 2006.

Lerangis, Peter. *Antarctica: Journey to the Pole* (Antarctica, 1). New York: Scholastic, 2000.

Mara, Wil. *The Seven Continents* (Rookie Read-About Geography). Danbury, CT: Children's Press, 2005.

Pipe, Jim. *The Race to the South Pole* (Stories from History). Grand Rapids, MI: School Specialty Publishing, 2006.

Scott, Elaine. *Poles Apart: Why Penguins and Polar Bears Will Never Be Neighbors.* New York: Viking Children's Books, 2004.

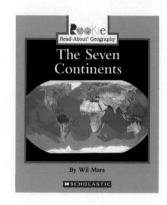

# Organizations and Web Sites

## Zoom School: Antarctica
www.enchantedlearning.com/school/Antarctica
Learn about snowflakes, meteorites, and dinosaurs
in Antarctica. Try some quizzes, and see Antarctica
from outer space.

## Discovering Antarctica
www.discoveringantarctica.org.uk/index.php
Take a journey of discovery through Antarctica,
with activities, images, video clips, and fact sheets.

## Welcome to Antarctica
http://astro.uchicago.edu/cara/vtour/
Take a cool, step-by-step virtual tour of Antarctica.

# Places to Visit

## Discovery Point
Discovery Quay
Dundee DD1 4XA
Scotland, U.K.
+44 (1382) 309 060
www.rrsdiscovery.com

## International Antarctic Center
38 Orchard Road
Christchurch, New Zealand
+64 (3) 353 7798
www.iceberg.co.nz

# Important Words

**algae** – rootless, plantlike living things that live in water or damp places

**aurora** (uh-ROAR-uh) – streams of colored light visible in the night sky above the North and South poles

**climate** – the usual pattern of weather in a place

**diatom** (DYE-uh-tom) – a tiny, simple plantlike marine organism

**ice shelf** – a huge area of ice that is attached to the land. From the sea, an ice shelf can look like a series of long, white cliffs.

**katabatic** (ka-tuh-BAH-tik) – relating to a cold, fast-moving wind that sweeps down off a glacier

**lichen** (LYE-ken) – a complex, plantlike organism made up of two simple organisms that grow together on rocks and trees

**liverwort** (LIV-er-wort) – a small, leafy plant, related to moss, that has hair-like roots

**ozone** – a form of oxygen in the atmosphere that shields Earth from harmful ultraviolet radiation

**peninsula** – a long piece of land almost surrounded by water

**solar wind** – a stream of charged particles from the sun

**Southern Hemisphere** (HEH-muhss-fear) – the half of Earth that is below the equator

**ultraviolet light** – a kind of light that cannot be seen by the human eye

# Index

Page numbers in **bold** indicate illustrations

# About the Author

Mel Friedman is an award-winning journalist and children's book author. He holds a B.A. in history from Lafayette College and four graduate degrees from Columbia University, including one in East Asian studies. He has written or co-written more than two dozen children's books, both fiction and non-fiction. He often works on projects with his wife, who is also a writer. They have a grown-up daughter, and take in the occasional stray dog.

**PHOTOGRAPHS**: Big Stock Photo: (© Jan Will, back cover; p. 34); Chris Danals/National Science Foundation (p. 15); Getty Images (p. 9; p. 30; p. 41); Ingram Publishing Ltd./*London Illustrated News* (p. 32); istockphoto.com (pp. 4–5; stamp, p. 35; p. 39); Maps.com (front cover); Photolibrary (pp. 26–29; p. 38); Stock.Xpert (p. 21); Tranz: (Corbis, p. 6; pp. 12–14; p. 16; pp. 19–20; pp. 22–24; p. 40; p. 42; Photoshot.com, p. 10; Popperfoto, p. 33); © Will Steger (p. 36); www.airforce.forces.gc.ca/En.wikipedia (plane, p. 35)

The publisher would like to thank Will Steger for the use of the photograph on page 36.